Home Burial

Books by Michael McGriff

Home Burial

Dismantling the Hills

Choke

The Sorrow Gondola, Tomas Tranströmer [translator, with
Mikaela Grassl]

*To Build My Shadow a Fire: The Poetry and Translations of
David Wevill* [editor]

Michael McGriff
Home Burial

Copper Canyon Press
Port Townsend, Washington

Cover art: James Everett Stanley, *070707*, watercolor, 16 x 19.5 inches

Copper Canyon Press is in residence at Fort Worden State Park in Port Townsend, Washington, under the auspices of Centrum. Centrum is a gathering place for artists and creative thinkers from around the world, students of all ages and backgrounds, and audiences seeking extraordinary cultural enrichment.

LIBRARY OF CONGRESS CATALOGING-IN-PUBLICATION DATA

McGriff, Michael, 1976–
  Home Burial / Michael McGriff.
    p. cm.
    ISBN 978-1-55659-384-0 (pbk.)
  1. Northwest, Pacific—Poetry. I. Title.
  PS3613.C4973H66 2012
  811'.6—dc23
                    2011043020

FIRST PRINTING

COPPER CANYON PRESS

Post Office Box 271
Port Townsend, Washington 98368
www.coppercanyonpress.org

Acknowledgments

Grateful acknowledgement is made to the editors of the books and periodicals in which these poems first appeared: "Catfish," "The Garments of the Night," "Invocation," "Note Left for My Former Self," and "The Residence of the Night" in *American Poetry Review;* "Above the Earth" and "Alone in Hell's Canyon" in *Bat City Review;* "My Family History as Explained by the South Fork of the River" in *The Believer;* "Year of the Rat" in *Cortland Review;* "In February," "Pipeline," and "Sunday" in *Indiana Review;* "Against My Will," "In the Break Room," and "Midwinter" in *The Missouri Review;* "All Dogs, You Said, Are Descendants of the Wolf," "The Cow," "Don't Explain," and "New Civilian" in *Narrative;* "The Book of Hours," "Dead Man's Bells, Witches' Gloves," and "Kissing Hitler" in *Neo* (Portugal); and "The Line between Heaven and Earth" in *Slate.*

"Drinking at the Rusted Oyster" first appeared in *Oyster Suite*, a fine-press edition with poems by Carl Adamshick, Matthew Dickman, and Michael Dickman (Charles Seluzicki Fine and Rare Books, 2011).

Special thanks to the Lannan Foundation for a Literary Fellowship and residency at Marfa that offered essential funding and artistic space. // Thanks to Jo Chapman. // Thanks to Michael Wiegers. // Thanks to Eavan Boland and the Stanford Creative Writing Program. // Thanks to James Everett Stanley. // Thanks to David Wevill, Sara Michas-Martin, Bruce Snider, and Andrew Grace for poring over this book in its earliest forms. // Thanks to Britta Ameel, Carl Adamshick, Michael Dickman, Matthew Dickman, Joseph Millar, and Dorianne Laux—ever faithful.

for Britta

Contents

Home Burial

...here comes midnight with the dead moon in its jaws...

—*Jason Molina*

Kissing Hitler

I've tried to keep the landscape
buried in my chest, in its teak box,
but tonight, awakened
by the sound of my name
strung between the trees,
I see the box on my nightstand
giving off the kind of light
you never know you belong to

until you see it dance
from a pile of metal shavings

or shaken loose
from a sword fern's root-wad.

It's the same light that trailed me
the entire summer of my sixteenth year,
driving County Road 64
toward Power Line Ridge,
the three radio towers
blinking in the Oregon dark.

Between each red pulse
the dark hung its birthrights in front of me,
a few dead branches
crawling up from the ditch,
a lost bolt of mooncloth
snagged on a barbed-wire fence,
shredding in the tide wind.

The light my oldest friends
slammed into their veins

or offered to the night
when they made amends.

One of them,
the tallest and toughest,
the one who used to show up Saturdays
for my mother's breakfast—
he could juggle five eggs
and recite the alphabet backward—
he told me as he covered my hand with his
while I downshifted to enter the gravel quarry
that he wanted to punch the baby
out of Jessica's stomach—

he's the one, tonight, whose carbide hands
have opened the lid of this little box.

I can see the two of us now, kissing Hitler.
That's what we called it—
siphoning gas,
huffing shop rags.

And we kissed him everywhere,
in other counties,
with girls we barely knew
telling us to hurry
before someone called the cops.

They can't arrest you for kissing Hitler.
That's what we said.

The last time I saw him
he sat on the edge

of his father's girlfriend's bathtub,
bleeding and laughing hard into a pink towel.

I can't remember—
maybe it was a birthday party.
Maybe we'd climbed in
through the living room window,
looking for a bottle or some pills,
at the same moment the adults stumbled in
from the Silver Dollar, hardwired
to liquor and crystal.

That was the summer
when people just went crazy.

And there we were, locked in the bathroom,
someone yelling and throwing themselves
against the door,
my friend's blood fanned out behind him
into points of red tar,

into points so fine they made me think
that someone, somewhere,
must belong to a family that passes down
the art of painting immaculate nasturtiums
along the lips of bone china,
the smallest detail touched into place
by a single, stiff horsehair,
by a young father holding his breath,
trying not to wake the child
swaddled at his feet, his hand

steady as five white mining burros
sleeping in the rain.

New Civilian

The new law
says you can abandon your child
in an emergency room,
no questions asked.

A young father
carries his sleeping boy
through the hospital doors.

Later, parked at the boat basin,
he takes a knife from his pocket,
cuts an unfiltered cigarette in two,
lights the longer half in his mouth.

He was a medic in the war.

In his basement are five bronze eagles
that once adorned the walls
of a dictator's palace.

Dead Man's Bells, Witches' Gloves

The dreams of those buried in winter
push through the ground in summer.

Among the orders, my dead
belong to the ditches of county roads.

Before the new people came over
to negotiate the easement
with their version of a city lawyer,
my mother hung dozens of foxgloves
above our door.

A dead crow hung by its feet
from the same hook.

Even in death, that purple luster
is a kind of singing.

Catfish

The catfish have the night,
but I have patience
and a bucket of chicken guts.
I have canned corn and shad blood.
And I've nothing better to do
than listen to the water's riffled dark
spill into the deep eddy
where a '39 Ford coupe
rests in the muck-bottom.

The dare growing up:
to swim down with pliers
for the license plates,
corpse bones, a little chrome…
But even on the clearest days,
even when the river runs low and clean,
you can't see it,
though you can often nearly see
the movement of hair.

I used to move through my days
as someone agreeable
to all the gears
clicking in the world.
I was a big clumsy Yes
tugged around by its collar.
Yes to the mill, yes to the rain,
yes to what passed
for fistfights and sex, yes
to all the pine boards of thought
waiting around for the hammer.

The catfish have the night
and ancient gear oil for blood,
they have a kind of greased demeanor
and wet electricity
that you can never boil out of them.

The catfish have the night,
but I have the kind of patience
born of indifference and hate.

Maybe the river and I share this.

Maybe the obvious moon
that bobs near the lip of the eddy
is really a pocket watch
having finally made its way downstream
from what must have been
a serious accident—
the station wagon and its family
busting the guardrail,
the steering wheel jumping
into the man's chest,
his pocket watch hurtling
through the windshield
and into the river.

Wind the hands in one direction
and see into the exact moment of your death.

Wind them the other way
and see all the tiny ways
you've already died—

for days at a time
and comes home ragged
and soaked with rainwater.
My mother has a special branch
that follows the water.

My grandfather says
I was never born at all,
that I'm just borrowing this body
until something better comes along.

He says I'm half bird
and half fish.

He says there's a house
beneath the river,
that I'm in a riddle
where a boy flies
in two skies at the same time.

In February

She looks at the apple trees
and imagines rows of people
standing in line for something.
She even dreamt once
of being among them,
waiting patiently to enter
the open doorway
of the earth, which shone
with a light so forgiving
it could have spoken.

Her son's been dead
nearly a year, and yesterday
while driving to the feed store
she braked suddenly
and threw her arm
across the rib cage
of his absence.

The ice grows down the ruts
of the gravel driveway.
The possum by the well
frozen in place
for over a week.
Wood smoke hangs
halfway up the trees,
the air is still.

Gunshots can be heard for miles,
and every kind of water
and laughter.

New Season

Beside our neighbor's half-framed barn
the hip bones of a dead deer continue
to be stripped and polished by the rain,
an arc of gray electricity
traveling between them.

And the water
collecting in the ashtray on the porch
isn't a lake, but it's big enough for God
to stick his thumb in.

I admire the rats in the wall.
They rejoice in the night.
They call to each other
as they work.

Sunday

Something anvil-like
something horselike
knee-deep and gleaming
in the flooded pasture.

The smell of fence posts and barn-rot.
Culverts and tow chains.

My mother and her illness.
My father and his patience.

My thoughts for them glow like quarry light.

I wish I were the proud worms
twisting out of nowhere
to writhe and thrash
as if their god had fulfilled
his promise.

In rooms all over town
the faithful raise their hands
to the gathering radiance

as I lower my head to the kitchen table
and listen to the black rails of December
bleeding into the distance.

Invocation

Out there, somewhere,
you are a variable
in the night's equation.

I listen hard
to the hands of smoke
moving beneath the river,

to the abandoned grain elevator
dragging its chains
through the tender blood
of the night.

I listen to the hush
of your name
as it's subtracted
from one darkness
then added to another.

＊

I pray to what you are not.

You are the opposite of a horse.
Your hair is not the seven colors
of cemetery grass.
Your mouth is not a dead moon,

nor is it the winter branches
preparing their skeletons
for the wind.

A double thread of darkness
winds through me,
and the night's coarse tongue
scrapes your name
against the trees.

❂

I've found a good spot by the river.

The trees line up along either bank
and bend toward the center.

I've been trying to get rid
of that part of myself
that I most despise
but need most to survive—
it rises like wood smoke,

it's shaped like a brass key,
and the hole it looks to enter
can be seen through,
revealing a banquet hall
with one chair
and countless silver trays
piled with rags.

❂

Is your voice in the linden
wood of an oar?

Your face in the daily ritual
of the Cooper's hawk?

Is your charity the green rot
of a fence post?

Are you near me
as I clean this ashtray
with my sleeve?

Are you the dead doe's skull
shining from within itself?—

I've been pretending
not to hear it speak to me,

even though I've entered its voice,
hung my coat
from a nail in its pantry

without bumping the table
or creaking the floor

and moved in the utter darkness of it.

✿

It's finally late enough
that all sounds
are the sounds of water.

If you die tonight
I'll wash your feet.

I'll remove the batteries
from the clocks.

And the two moths
that drown in the lakes
of your eyes
will manage the rest.

Year of the Rat

I winch up the sky
between the shed roof and the ridge
and stand dumb as a goat
beneath its arrows and buckets,
its harmonies and hungers.

Each night I feel a speck of fire
twisting in my gut,
and each night
I ask the Lord
the same questions,

and by morning the same
spools of barbed wire
hang on the barn wall
above footlockers of dynamite.

We used to own everything
between the river and the road.

We bought permits
for home burials
and kept a horse's skull above the door.

We divided the land,
we filled in the wells,
we spit in the river,
we walked among the cows
and kept the shovels sharp.

Tonight I'm sitting
on the back porch

of the universe
in the first dark hours
of the Year of the Rat.
I'm tuned in to AM 520
and, depending
on how intently I stare
into the black blooms of the sky,
it bounces either
to a high school football game
or to the voices of rage,
of plague and prophecy.

The wind off the river
is weak and alone, like the voice
of my brother.
He's trying to melt the plastic coating
from a stolen bundle
of commercial wiring,
a black trickle of smoke
winding through his body
to empty itself into a pool
that shimmers with the ink of nothing.

If I had faith in the stars
I'd let those four there
be the constellation of my brother
lying flat on the ground, asking for money.

I like the song
he almost sings,
the one he doesn't know the words to
but hums to himself

in these few moments
of absolute stillness.

And I like how he's resting
with his hands under his head
as he stretches out
among the dark echoes
and spindled light
of all that black wheat.

Symphony

It rained all night, hard,
the constant hum
like an orchestra tuning up,
its members taking purposeful,
deep breaths.

When I closed my eyes
I saw my father
unstacking and restacking
an empire of baled hay,

heaving his days
into the vagaries
of chaff-light.

The conductor raises his arms,
whispers a quick prayer
in a foreign tongue,
then begins.

To the Woman Whose Waist-Long Hair Lowered Itself into My Dream for the Third Night in a Row

When she stepped down from her pickup
and spilled her purse onto the blacktop,
the pills from an orange
pint-sized prescription bottle scattered
and began melting in the rain.

She knelt there,
the tungsten-gray streaks in her hair
indistinguishable
from the paths the pills cut,
bleeding across the parking lot.

Overhearing Two Sisters in the Empty Lot behind the DMV

—It's my turn.

    —Make the worst face you've ever made.

—You look like you're dead.

    —You look like a ghost who can't shit.

—Let's pretend we were murdered.

    —Let's do one with our mouths open.

Midwinter

Midwinter.
She lets the darkness
sit down beside her.
Some nights
she walks through the pasture
and out of her body.
Some nights she sits
in the Studebaker
junked by the millpond
and dials through the radio,
the electricity of Jupiter
hijacking the AM frequencies
with its ocean sounds,
its static code, a coyote
whose mouth is stuffed
with volts and rust.
Tonight she sits at the kitchen table.
She could be over the bay,
high enough to see
that it's shaped like a rabbit
hanging limp
from the jaws of the landscape.
She hasn't spoken
in days—she's afraid
what comes alive at night
will break if she talks about it.
The wives of the Legionnaires
bring her food once a week,
and a Bible the size
of a steam iron.

She packs up her china
each afternoon,
then unpacks it before bed.

She could be flying
the way it looks
with all this fog gusting by.

Note Left for My Former Self

I've seen a group of farm kids
hypnotize a rabbit
by pinning it on its back
then stroking its neck.

This is what I think of
when I see you in the night—

not the trick,
but the distress call
we manage to send out
while we are pinned
to our stillness.

The Cow

I used to think of this creek as a river
springing from mineral caverns
of moonmilk and slime,

but really it's just a slow thread of water
that comes from somewhere up north
to trickle its way out
near the edge of our property.

And I've always imagined
the toolshed as it is,
though it was once
an outbuilding for a watermill
whose wheel and timbers
have been reborn
as exposed rafters and flooring
for the Old Money in the valley.

The day before my grandfather died
he drove a diesel flatbed
to the edge of the creek
and paid ten day laborers
to unload this shed.

He left his will on the shed floor,
which wasn't a will
as much as it was a quick note
scrawled on the pink edge of an invoice
for a few bundles of chicken wire.

I found the note
and showed it to no one.

This shed should have the smell
of seed packets and mousetraps.
It should have a calendar
whose pages haven't turned since Truman.

The sounds of usefulness and nostalgia
should creak from its hinges,
but instead there's nothing
but a painting the size of a dinner plate
that hangs from an eightpenny nail,
a certain style of painting
where the wall of a building
has been lifted away
to reveal the goings-on of each room,
which, in this case, is a farmhouse
where some men and women
sit around the geometry
of a kitchen table playing pinochle,
a few of the women laughing
a feast-day kind of laughter,
and one of the men, a fat one
in overalls with a quick brushstroke
for a mouth, points up
as if to say something
about death or the rain
or the reliable Nordic construction
of the rafters.

A few of the children
gathered in a room off to one side
have vaguely religious faces—
they're sitting on the floor around their weak
but dependable uncle

who plays something festive
on the piano. The piano
next to the fireplace, the fireplace lit,
a painting of the farmhouse
hanging above the mantel.

What passes for middle C
ripples away from the uncle, the children,
the pinochle game—
the wobbling note finally collapsing
in the ear of the cow
standing in perfect profile
at the far right of the painting.

The cow faces east and stands knee-deep
in pasture mud. The pasture
is a yellow, perspectiveless square,
and the cow, if you moved her
inside the house, would stand
with the sway of her back
touching the rafters.
Perhaps the fat man is referring
to the impossibility of it all,
the inevitable disproportion,
the slow hiss of something he can't explain.

The cow is gray and blue
and orange. This is the cow
that dies in me every night,
the one that doesn't sleep
standing up, or sleep at all,
but stamps through the pasture muck
just to watch the suckholes she makes

fill with a salty rot-water
that runs a few inches
below the surface of everything here.

The cow noses through
the same weak spot in the same fence,
and every night finds herself
moving out beyond the field of her dumb,
sleeping sisters.

The cow in me has long admired
the story the night tells itself,
the one with rifle shots and laughter,
gravel roads crunching under pickups
with their engines and lights cut,
the story with the owls
diving through the circles
their iron silences
scratch into the air.

The cow in me never makes it past
the edge of the painting—
and she's not up to her knees in mud,
she's knee-deep in a cattle guard.
Bone and hoof and hoods of skin
dangle below the steel piping
into the clouds of the underworld.

The cow cries, and her cry
slits the night open and takes up house.
The cry has a blue interior
and snaps like a bonfire stoked
with dry rot and green wood.

The cry is a pitcher of ink that never spills,
until it does, until it scrawls itself
across the fields and up into the trees.

The cry works in the night
like a dated but efficient system.

The cry becomes a thread of black water
where the death-fish spawn.

On nights like this
the cow inside me cries,
and I wake as the cry leaves my mouth
to find its way back to the shed,
where it spreads
through all the little rooms of the painting
like the heat building up
from the fireplace by the piano.

The cry makes a little eddy
around the fat man's finger.

It turns the pinochle deck
into the sounds of the creek
trickling into nothing.

The cry watches my grandfather
weeping over the only thing
he said to my father
in two decades,
which he didn't say at all
but penned onto a crumpled invoice
that found its way to the nowhere
of my hands.

The cry in the cow
in the painting in me
rotates in the night
on a long axle of pain,
and the night itself
has no vanishing point.

All Dogs, You Said, Are Descendants of the Wolf

Luis, they dragged their hooks
through the slough for your body.

You would've liked how it snowed
on the rescue team, the searchlights
shining into the easiness of all that white
entering the water,
the smoke of drag slicks
entering the darkness.

Your laugher was ridiculous and certain
and swirled around you
like the ravens of luck.

You're still out there
in the orchard-light of August.

You've just been thrown
from your uncle's horse.

You're picking gravel from your knees,
shaking the dust from the black wings
of your happiness.

The lamp you left in me
has enough oil to last the winter.

Saint Luis, Protector of Horse Thieves,
beholden to nothing
but the wild dog in the moon.

Crows

Nine varieties of crows
whoop and gnash
in my bloodstream.

I'm overcome with nine
particular kinds of joy
as I cross under the power lines
along the rail yard.

The tracks touch in the horizon,
forming the tip of an exquisite beak.

Circadian

A farmhouse, burned down
for the insurance money,
stood where my life had been.

By then a cold seam of daylight
ran through the trees.

Star-still in that early hour,
a fence-hawk
began to fill with tar

as it looked across
the glittering, overfished river.

Alone in Hell's Canyon

Out here in the desert
I smell smoke from a fire someone made
thinking he had the exclusive company
of the wildflowers
that bloom every hundred years.

Perhaps he too awakened last night
to the noise of a grand floating hall
where an entire people
was celebrating.

One person had the job
of tending thousands of chandelier candles.

I listened to him drag his ladder
from one to another, hour after hour.

The Line between Heaven and Earth

The line between heaven and earth
glows just slightly
when a bear's gallbladder
is hacked out and put on ice
in California.

The gallbladder rides
in a foam cooler
on a bench seat
in a pickup heading north.

The line between heaven and earth
carries a crate of dried fish on its back.

The man driving the gallbladder
used to sell Amway
and sand dollars blessed
by Guatemalan priests.

The crate of fish
also contains the stars,
which do not spill out
above the truck stop
on the Oregon side
of the border,
where one man
counts another's money,
and the gallbladder passes hands.

This is my father,
who drove two days
to spend all the borrowed money

he could find,
who unpacks the organ,
lets it warm on a tin sheet
above his Buick's engine block
before he crushes
an ashy powder into the bile
and spoons it
into the mouth of a child
whose shallow breaths
become the music of blood
riding the updrafts
of the foothills.

Pipeline

On the new calendar,
on a day no one cares about,
I wake with the taste
of galvanized nails in my mouth.

The fog tumbles off the bay,
and those who hunger
for a clean shave and fortune
prepare their strategies
for the pipeline
that will tear through our acreage,
a ninety-foot clear-cut swath,
hundreds of miles long,
suits and easy money.

A thin white noise hissing
at the back of everything—
even my boots carry the sound,
even the chimney caps,
a drawer full of bobbins,
a chipped pint glass
and its mineral-brown water.

During these last weeks of summer
I get shuffled
from one day to the next
like a tin bucket
passed along a fire line,
the water slopping out,
never quite reaching the barn
or the dusty horses.

I want the music of Eric Dolphy
to drift above the land surveyors
triangulating the west side
of our property, that brass tangle,
that shot glass full of eels.

I want Tarkovsky
to show them the apocalypse
in a pitcher of milk.

The summer's out there
crashing through its own trees,
breaking its spine.
The wheat growing near our fence
turns to long, ordinary grass.

If you looked into my eyes right now
you'd see the gray drone
of Ocean Avenue
and the white sails
the dead hoist.
You'd see the landscape
spinning like a compass needle
above the dirt of a new grave.

You'd see a group of men
huddled around a fire
discussing what they'll buy
with the checkbook they found
in an abandoned tract house—

the smoke rising into the air
as if something significant
were about to happen,

as if the day isn't being ground
to a fine powder
by the gears of an elegant pepper mill
resting on the glassy black table
of this new century.

Above the Earth

The volunteer firemen take turns
tapping the stone chimney
on the dead man's farmhouse
with crowbars and flashlights.

They've determined the only way
to remove the body: topple the chimney,
cut a hole in the second story,
borrow Peterson's crane for the rest.

They'll need tow straps and come-alongs.
They'll need to lower him
to a flatbed truck, then ratchet him down
beneath a blue tarp.

They'll do the best they can.

The obituary won't mention
his collection of state fair thimbles
or glass hummingbirds,
or how the crane swung his five hundred pounds
out over his own land
where the grasses stood tall
then bent toward the river

as sparks fell from the jaws of the cows
chewing the evening
down to its bright roots.

Drinking at the Rusted Oyster

Whitecaps in the harbor,
the color of a dead cow's eye
the moment it breaks its orbit
from the skull.

Trollers buck against their moorings,
and the afternoon has a voice
like a woodshed full of dead lawn chairs,

a voice like my mother's nail polish
and my father's lottery tickets.

All the tired arguments are wind-ripped
from the bones of salt,
and we enter those arguments.

I'm terrified of old acquaintances.
I'm eating Angels on Horseback.
I'm drinking a glass of light.

The Residence of the Night

It's always night inside the whales—

even when they heave themselves
onto the shore
where they death-hiss, wheeze,
and balloon with gas—

even when we dynamite them
back into the night.

The night inside a barn owl's wing-hush
is the handshake
of a secret order.

It's inside the way
we pass one another
at the grocery store,
the feed lot, the way
we lower our wet ropes
into each other.

It's night inside the peacocks,
whose cries cut through us
like the prow of a ship
whose cauldrons of whale oil
shine their darkness up
to the floating ribs of the moon.

It's in the way we tend
to the churches of our skulls,
where the night swings

its smoking chains
and arranges its candles.

The tractor, of course,
is filled with it.
It won't start
until you summon
the lampblack
in the river of your blood,
where the sturgeon
are decimal points
moving upstream
zero by zero.

The Book of Hours

The first time I handled a snake
I picked up what I mistook
for a husk of shed skin.

I lifted it high
into the barn's dust-tipped heat.

The hay bales trembled
as I pressed my lips
to its hinge of light,

the eternal mathematics
of its living head.

Don't Explain

Don't explain the black donkeys in the desert
or the sound of water beneath me
when I stopped to watch them.

Don't explain the night, its rifled dark,
the moon spinning through its chamber.

Don't explain the wounded alphabet
dragging itself through the groves of ash.

When George died, twelve dusty hours
were filled with the noise of a horse
rubbing its side against the old barn,

the lighting rod's glass globe
shifting from white to green.

George Hitchcock, 1914–2010

In the Break Room

The mill holds us
in its mouth,
the graveyard shift
and its floodlights.

There's a stillness between us
as we eat our sandwiches
and leftovers.

Back in town
someone's daughter
stays up all night
eating her own hair.
A woman on Third Street
applies makeup to a corpse
she's recently washed.
A cop drifts over a fog line
in his Crown Victoria.

Todd thinks the foreman's
new girlfriend looks
like a country singer,
her hair shines
like broken glass.
She rests her hand
on the animal of sleep
and it leans against her leg.

In fifteen minutes
she'll crawl up a ladder
into a metal cage

where hot sheets of plywood
shoot out one after another
like a satanic card trick,
and she'll guide them
by the edge, in midair,
and let them drop
to the sorter…

until she closes her eyes
just long enough
to float upon the waters
where sleep winds
through the cattails.

When a sheet of veneer
tears her face open
a corpse's hands
will be placed together,
the cop will drive
his cruiser into the river,
which will soon fill
with a daylight our curses
may never reach.

The Light in November

The days in their damp, cold eternities.
Gravel roads corkscrewing past haylofts,
skulls that buck in the shore wind,
a few ghosts testing their ropes.

The Lucky Logger Diner
stands where the pavement ends
and the gravel begins.
Above my favorite booth,
the portrait of Lewis and Clark
our mayor painted for the county fair.

I like it when the light sits beside me.
Even the light in November
that staggers behind my father
as he walks home from the cannery,
pausing in the middle of the bridge
to watch a gravel barge
lower its boom into the river.

The piece of him the season will take
drifts out into the dead-letter office
of the evening air, and the light passes,
brushing his sleeve.

The Garments of the Night

The night undresses.
Its clothes, strewn
across the fields
and over the houses,

begin to pile high
where the creek spills
into the green gears
of the lake.

I'll pull the dark thread of my faith
until whatever it holds together

falls into a gulch
of black stars

where some buzzards
unravel the dead,

placing each strand
on a stretch of river rocks
still warm to the touch.

Against My Will

Against my will
I am reborn as a bird
who claws its way
from the throat
of a man

who never cared
for the moth-light of August,

who never read
the cosmologies of rain
or the doctrines of silt,

who never walked
into the static death-light
the goats tear away
from the clover,

a man who bled himself
of axle grease
keno tickets
and county roads
named for men
whose legacies
are Stop signs raddled
in buckshot
and gray light.

The night
keeps painting its tongue black,
and I am reborn
as a bird who flies

from the throat of a man
who gives no thought
to January's frozen
moon-crush
twisting the alder branches
from their trees.

Against my will I am reborn
into a land stretched flat

and bled of its salt and black ice,
of its choked roots and bird's blood
looped through the eyelets
of the southerly winds.

I am reborn as a denier
of barn dust
pinion moans
stolen hand tools
and chipped dishes.

I am reborn with no thought
for the river's breath
pulling a tune
through the cathedral ribs
of a common rat.

I am reborn as one free
of reduction gears
ash buckets
green sparks
analog currents
amphetamines
pounding inside

the stubborn machine
of the horse's skull.

I am reborn
into the darkest hour
and its search parties,

their flashlights dimming
as the morning
brightens the room
where I am reborn as a bird

who claws its way
from the throat
of a man
who wears my name
for a face

and the heavy jewels
of compliance
around his wrist.

I fly through the window
of his voice
and make my way
to the edge
of the continent
where the scrubtrees
cower from the shore

and I discover
like the trees here

it's against my nature
to look out
over the sea.

Salt-disasters rage
and burn the feathers
on my back.

I open my mouth

and it's the man's voice
calling me home.

Notes

The epigraph "…here comes midnight with the dead moon in its jaws…" is taken from Jason Molina's song "Farewell Transmission" on his Songs: Ohia album *Magnolia Electric Co.* (Secretly Canadian, 2003).

"The Cow" is for David Wevill.

"All Dogs, You Said, Are Descendants of the Wolf" is based on James Everett Stanley's painting *070707*.

About the Author

Michael McGriff was born and raised in Coos Bay, Oregon. His books include *Dismantling the Hills; To Build My Shadow a Fire: The Poetry and Translations of David Wevill;* and a co-translation of Tomas Tranströmer's *The Sorrow Gondola.* His poetry, translations, and essays have appeared in numerous publications, including *American Poetry Review, Bookforum, Slate, Narrative, The Believer,* and *The Wall Street Journal.* He has received a Lannan Literary Fellowship, a Stegner Fellowship, and a National Endowment for the Arts Literary Fellowship. He is the founding editor of Tavern Books, a publishing house devoted to poetry in translation and the reviving of out-of-print books.

Lannan Literary Selections

For two decades Lannan Foundation has supported the publication
and distribution of exceptional literary works. Copper Canyon Press
gratefully acknowledges their support.

LANNAN LITERARY SELECTIONS 2012

Matthew Dickman and Michael Dickman, *50 American Plays*

Michael McGriff, *Home Burial*

Tung Hui-Hu, *Greenhouses, Lighthouses*

James Arthur, *Charms Against Lightning*

Natalie Diaz, *When My Brother Was an Aztec*

RECENT LANNAN LITERARY SELECTIONS FROM COPPER CANYON PRESS

Michael Dickman, *Flies*

Laura Kasischke, *Space, In Chains*

Deborah Landau, *The Last Usable Hour*

Sarah Lindsay, *Twigs and Knucklebones*

Heather McHugh, *Upgraded to Serious*

W.S. Merwin, *Migration: New & Selected Poems*

Valzhyna Mort, *Collected Body*

Taha Muhammad Ali, *So What: New & Selected Poems, 1971-2005*,
translated by Peter Cole, Yahya Hijazi, and Gabriel Levin

Lucia Perillo, *Inseminating the Elephant*

Ruth Stone, *In the Next Galaxy*

John Taggart, *Is Music: Selected Poems*

Jean Valentine, *Break the Glass*

C.D. Wright, *One Big Self: An Investigation*

Dean Young, *Fall Higher*

For a complete list of Lannan Literary Selections from
Copper Canyon Press, please visit Partners on our Web site:
www.coppercanyonpress.org

Since 1972, Copper Canyon Press has fostered the work of emerging, established, and world-renowned poets for an expanding audience. The Press thrives with the generous patronage of readers, writers, booksellers, librarians, teachers, students, and funders — everyone who shares the belief that poetry is vital to language and living.

MAJOR SUPPORT HAS BEEN PROVIDED BY:

THE PAUL G. ALLEN
FAMILY FOUNDATION

amazon.com

the
POINT
WHERE LESS IS MORE

golden
lasso

Lannan

THE MAURER FAMILY
FOUNDATION

NATIONAL
ENDOWMENT
FOR THE ARTS

WASHINGTON STATE
ARTS COMMISSION

The Paul G. Allen Family Foundation
Amazon.com
Anonymous
Arcadia Fund
John Branch
Diana and Jay Broze
Beroz Ferrell & The Point, LLC
Mimi Gardner Gates
Carolyn and Robert Hedin
Golden Lasso, LLC
Gull Industries, Inc.
on behalf of William and Ruth True
Lannan Foundation
Rhoady and Jeanne Marie Lee
Maurer Family Foundation
National Endowment for the Arts
New Mexico Community Foundation
Penny and Jerry Peabody
Joseph C. Roberts
Cynthia Lovelace Sears and Frank Buxton
Washington State Arts Commission
Charles and Barbara Wright

To learn more about underwriting Copper Canyon Press titles,
please call 360-385-4925 ext. 103

The Chinese character for poetry is made up of two parts:
"word" and "temple." It also serves as pressmark for Copper
Canyon Press.

The poems are set in New Caledonia.
Book design and composition by Phil Kovacevich.
Printed on archival-quality paper at McNaughton & Gunn, Inc.